T0068232

Thoughts for leading a successful life are presented with a view to using the criteria and elements of a successful life. It was found that the individual must acquire and possess a basic education with emphasis on knowledge and values to earn a living for himself, his family, society, and mankind. The individual should also overcome difficulties in his endeavors, such as rejection and the absence of recognition. The individual must also strive to succeed with his family, ensuring a stable and supportive family environment.

A special section is provided to review and discuss the impact of a recently developed computer-based science, Artificial Intelligence (AI), on a successful life.

This book was primarily written for

(1) Psychology and sociology professionals to provide thoughts and a simple model for a successful life.
(2) Individuals with interests in learning about a successful life and its components.
(3) Individuals with interests in considering what a professional life is or is not.
(4) Individuals with an interest in leading a successful life.
(5) Individuals interested in learning about possible impacts of AI on a successful life.

Finally, this book should be considered evolutionary since it is based on current available information to develop and apply a model relevant for understanding and assessing a successful life. A revision or a refinement of some elements of the model and its applications is warranted as more information becomes available.

Introduction

Life is the most precious gift that is given to us at birth. It is therefore important for us to preserve this gift and ensure that we live our life to the fullest, in a manner that we enjoy and cherish to achieve our objectives, whatever they may be.

We first attempt to define and rationalize the nature and various aspects of a successful life. Elements of success are identified, and the effects of acceptance and recognition of the individual are analyzed. The key questions of "who is to decide if a life is successful or not?" and "why do we need a successful life?" are examined (Chapter 2).

Life success is represented by a simple model that includes absolute, relative, and personal criteria, or a combination thereof. These criteria are identified and discussed (Chapter 3).

The elements of success in life are further reviewed and include focus, goals, and achievements.

Acceptance is the next step toward success and includes social, political, legal, and economic components. Recognition which represents a higher level of acceptance is also discussed (Chapter 4).

The various levels of success that can be reached include performance, fulfillment, accomplishment, achievement, exploit, and triumph. These levels are followed by the stage of "beyond success" that the individual must face after success has been reached. The roles of money and power in assessing the value of one's success are discussed (Chapter 5).

Cases of successful and unsuccessful lives are presented and analyzed (Chapter 6).

Thoughts for leading a successful life are presented with a view to using the basic elements and criteria of a successful life (Chapter 7).

A special section is provided to review and discuss the impact of Artificial Intelligence (AI) on a successful life (Section 8.0) with specific considerations for the impact of AI on success criteria, the elements of success, the levels of success, and the roles of money and power.

Thoughts on how to have a successful life with AI are presented (Section 9.0).

A Successful life: What and Why?

2.1 What is a successful life?

Everyone's life is precious and must be lived to its fullest. It is therefore important to define success in life or, more precisely, what constitutes a successful life.

A successful life is a life where the individual has used or is using specific criteria to live a meaningful life of defined goals and accomplishments. The criteria used may be absolute as prescribed by a divine influence, relative as set by social norms, needs, and objectives, or personal as set and inspired by the individual's values and motivation. A successful life may also be motivated by the combination of absolute, relative, and personal criteria.

The elements of success consist of focus, goals, and achievements. To achieve success the individual relies on education, knowledge, and integrity which are essential to the individual's judgment and self-confidence. Key external factors to be considered include regulatory, social, political, legal, and environmental factors that influence the individual.

Can a life be successful without acceptance and recognition? The answer to this question is complex since acceptance and recognition are essential to acknowledge that a life has been successful with respect to the norms of society. However, one may argue that indeed life can be successful as measured objectively by accomplishments and achievements alone.

The level of success achieved may be measured by contributions to society or by money earned by the individual. However, this level of success is expected to be limited until acceptance and recognition of the individual have occurred. The individual may also be characterized as unsuccessful although his or her achievements have been demonstrated and money was earned. In this case, a limited success was reached as measured by money, but without recognition by society.

In many cases, indeed, a high level of success may be achieved in life as achievements and accomplishments are fully accepted and recognized. Money may or may not be a factor, since in this case success may be achieved independently of money.

Another important question is: "who is to decide if a life was successful or not?". The answer to this question lies in the success criteria used to assess the success of the individual's life. If absolute criteria are used to judge the success of one's life, the decision must be made according to compliance with divine criteria, such as strict adherence to divine laws and commandments. If relative criteria are used to assess the success of one's life, the decision must be made according to the contributions of the individual to society in areas such as military, professional, scientific, financial, political, legal, or spiritual, and the level of recognition of these contributions by the people affected. In this case the people affected judge the success achieved by the individual. Following the affected people's death, ultimately, history makes a final judgment with respect to the individual successful life.

If personal criteria are used to judge the success of one's life, the decision may be made by the people affected by the successful individual. These people may or may not provide an objective judgment as the decision may be more personal and dependent on the level of acceptance or recognition of the successful individual. Other factors may also be used to assess the individual's success, such as personal relations, indoctrination, ideology, etc...

2.2 Why a successful life?

A successful life is a life that must be motivated and inspired by principles to live to meet divine, social, or personal requirements of achievements and accomplishments. Such a life is characterized by a strong sense of dedication to the benefit of society and personal purposes. The need for a successful life is recognized by the individual who understands that life must not be wasted and should convey clear messages of accomplishments and success. A successful life is a life that must be lived with the ultimate purpose to benefit society as a whole. Such a life stands beyond a purely biological life where species survival and biological well-being are the only goals. A successful life is a life of dedication that must be accepted by the people with a clear acknowledgment of the achievements provided. Such achievements may be professional, scientific, military, artistic, political, religious, or spiritual.

A successful life of dedication to the people is not a life of selfishness, hedonism, pleasure, or idleness. Instead, it may be inspired by work, devotion, prayer, meditation, or spiritual leadership.

A successful life is a life that brings a strong inspirational message to the people in exchange of acceptance and recognition by the people.

The Success Criteria

The success criteria for a successful life include the absolute criteria, the relative criteria, a combination of the absolute and relative criteria, and personal criteria. These criteria are graphically represented in Exhibit 1 and are reviewed below.

3.1 Absolute Success Criteria

The absolute criteria can be exemplified by the case of the political statesman that has made several decisions in the best interests of his country. The statesman had to analyze the political situation, review the political and military data, and select the option judged to be the most suitable for his country.

The political option selected has proved over the years to be the best option in terms of the interests and political goals of the statesman's country.

The military objectives have been met and even exceeded as the enemy was defeated and had to retreat. Moreover, the political objectives have been reached as the majority of the legislative branch of the government voted in favor of a resolution supporting the government's decision. The statesman was recognized as a great leader and was rewarded with re-election.

This represents the case of a successful statesman that led a successful life with a favorable outcome. The statesman had a very positive impact on the history of his country. The statesman was recognized as having made substantial contributions to his country to deserve the merit and honor of his accomplishments.

At first the life of the statesman could be considered successful considering all his successful achievements for the benefit of his country. History has also shown so.

On the other hand, however, the successful life of this statesman also included decisions that he made that cost the lives of hundreds of thousands of people as their houses and assets were also destroyed or damaged. This statesman was also able to suppress dissent in his country by eliminating his political opponents.

The question therefore remains: "Was the statesman life successful?"

The answer to this question is not straightforward as it depends on who is being asked.

One side will say that the statesman had a very successful life whereas the other side will claim that the statesman life could not have been successful since the statesman was viewed as a dictator with blood on his hands.

This case shows that an absolute criterion alone cannot be applied to judge the statesman's life successfulness. Instead, a relative criterion relevant to the statesman country and people must be applied.

The absolute criteria for a successful life, however, are characterized by absolute characteristics that refer to a divine presence and power that directly or indirectly influences the individual in life and guides him in his accomplishments.

The individual may be influenced by a divine presence and force that is exerted to accomplish specific tasks to the benefit of specific people or the whole community. God would prescribe strict and clear commandments for the individual to obey. The individual would follow the commandments based on his early vocation in life, his dedication to God, and his religious values and principles. The individual's vocation and dedication to a religious life is due to his entire inspiration and dedication to God and to God's revelation to him. It is with the set of God's commandments that the individual will accomplish in life and achieve success. The individual will realize that his success is God's will and that he played the role of an emissary dedicated to obeying and implementing God's commandments.

According to the philosopher Sponville (Ref. 1), absolute criteria are characterized by

- Eternity where no limits in time for the success criteria is applied.
- Infinity that characterizes success with the absence of space limits.
- The absolute where divine or superpowered criteria are used to measure success with absolute qualities of perfection or supernatural phenomena.

3.2 Relative Success Criteria

Relative success criteria are criteria of success that relate mostly to the power and influence that is acquired by individuals that emerge from the people as authorities, influencers, and leaders. Their success is measured directly relative to the people that have promoted them as leaders through acceptance and recognition.

Military power is probably the most structured form of power distributed and exerted at different levels. Military power relies on military force over individuals, people, and even civilizations. In general, this type of power does not need any ideology and support from the people as it does not necessarily rely on democratic processes. Instead, military power relies on the sheer force of weapons to influence and subjugate people. People will respect and obey military power under any specific rules that the military prescribe and implement for any length of time. In fact, history has shown that military power does not include a specific dimension of time as it can be exerted for any period.

Professional power is a form of power that derives from professional management and leadership. This power is exerted under the form of structured management of people in an organization. Although professional power may rely on skills and leadership, it is often exerted through management that is based on political skills, efficient communication, and networking. This form of power is intimately related to the character and egocentricity of a leader who is rewarded with the power to lead and make all kinds of professional and management decisions for the organization. Professional power, as a form of professional success, may be limited in time, depending on the management performance of the organization.

Financial power is a form of success where financial experts exert power through their businesses and companies using financial and economic means to market goods and services. Financial power relies essentially on financial means, but also allows to purchase or sell other forms of tools for military and political purposes.

Financial power stems from financial resources and thus has "staying power" if the financial resources are available. Through judicial financial decisions that include planning and control, financial power may therefore be limited in time.

Legal power is a form of success that is due to judicial power where legislators, magistrates, justices, and other legal experts exert power and oversight over the other branches of government. This form of power is derived mostly from the strict application and interpretation of laws. This form of success and legal power is limited in time as elected officials face term limitations. In other cases, certain government officials, such as justices, wield legal power for life.

Spiritual power is a form of success where religious or social leaders exert power on people through their religious and spiritual authority and leadership using religious and social principles and ideology. Spiritual power is usually exerted by a single or a group of religious leaders with unchallenged spiritual and moral authority relying solely on religious precepts and directives to influence and control the lives of other people.

Spiritual authority is usually based on immutable religious commandments and laws. This authority may be exerted in every aspect of life and does not have any time limitation, i.e., it can be exerted indefinitely.

According to the philosopher Sponville (Ref.1), relative criteria are characterized by

- The present that provides current conditions of time.
- Dimensional limits in space.
- Relativity where criteria of success are applied relative to humans.

3.3 Personal Criteria

The personal criteria for a successful life are unique in that they cannot be categorized as absolute, relative, or a combination of these two criteria. Instead, personal criteria for a successful life are characterized by personal traits of character, qualities (or shortfalls), and very personal focus and goals set by the individual.

Important traits of character that allow the individual to develop personal criteria of success and focus on his goals to be reached during his lifetime include:

- Loneliness
- Strong sense of observation
- Initiative
- Creativity
- Curiousness (Ref. 2)
- Concentration (Ref. 2)
- Perseverance (Ref. 2)
- Self-Critique (critically examining oneself) (Ref. 2)
- Trustful in one's personal judgment
- Self-control of emotions
- Capability to face challenges
- Adaptability

The individual sets his goals based on intimate personal conviction that these goals must be reached during his lifetime. Nothing will stop the individual from achieving his goals since they are paramount to any other considerations. These goals have been set based on the individual's pride and ego and reflect personal values that may also include elements of absolute and relative success criteria.

Personal criteria for a successful life may be surprising or unpredictable as they are based on the values, inspiration, and goals of the individual. The individual is totally polarized into his goals and onto the way to reach them. The individual may have some elements of absolute and relative criteria in his motivation to achieve a successful life. The goals of the individual, however, may be either beneficial or detrimental to the people affected or to mankind. This stems from the unpredictability of his personal criteria, as his criteria for a successful life may not be aligned with the best interests of the people. Furthermore, the achievements of the individual's life may not be accepted or recognized by the people. Nevertheless, the individual will move forward towards his goals as he remains fully motivated by his personal criteria.

As an example, Louis Pasteur (1822-1895) was a great chemist and microbiologist. He had a very successful life making significant progress in vaccine sciences and biology. He was recognized by the whole community as a great scientist and contributor to science and mankind. His goals and accomplishments were based on his professional, scientific, and personal values that he directed to the benefit of mankind. The community and he himself considered his life to be very successful.

Adolf Hitler (1889-1945) on the other hand was a politician that led Germany for twelve years that included World War II. He had extremely personal criteria for a successful life. He published his ideas, motivation, and philosophy in Mein Kampf (Ref. 6). He was viewed by his contemporary people as a great leader. However, as it turned out, Germany was defeated and was in ruins after World War II. Hitler, the German leader who was motivated by personal criteria for people annihilation and total destruction, is now viewed as having had a very unsuccessful life not only for himself but for the German people and his country as a whole.

He is judged by history as a failed leader, although during his time, he considered himself a successful leader according to his personal criteria.

3.4 Discussion

Based on the success model reviewed in the preceding sections, interesting observations can be made by considering the success criteria shown in Exhibit 1.

1. An individual can live only with absolute criteria of success (with no intersection with relative and personal criteria domains, see Exhibit 1). In this case the individual success is only determined by his adherence to God's laws and commandments, divine influence, and power. There is no concern whatsoever with relative criteria, where success is measured by professional impact on people. Similarly, the individual does not intend to

use any of his own values, inspiration, or personal interests and goals to achieve success.

As an example, this type of success is achieved by religious leaders who rely solely on implementation and strict compliance with religious laws and principles.

2. An individual can live only with relative criteria of success (with no intersection with absolute and personal criteria domains, see Exhibit 1). In this case, the individual success is only determined by his occupation or profession (such as managerial, military, financial, legal, spiritual, and others) that has been selected within rational limits of space and time and to the service of people and mankind. In this case, the individual's success is only determined by his adherence to his professional requirements to achieve success. There is no concern whatsoever with absolute criteria, where success is measured by religious laws or divine influence. Similarly, the individual does not intend to use any of his own values, inspiration, or personal interests and goals to achieve success.

    As an example, this type of success is achieved by eminent scientists, military leaders, financial and legal experts, spiritual leaders, philosophers, etc.

3. An individual can live only with personal criteria of success (with no intersection with absolute and relative criteria domains, see Exhibit 1). In this case the individual's success is only determined by personal criteria (that may be unpredictable) since they are based on the personal values, inspiration, interests, and goals of the individual. In this case, the individual's success is only determined by his strict adherence to his personal values and goals to achieve success. The individual has no concern whatsoever with absolute criteria where success is measured by religious laws or divine influence. Also, the individual does not

intend to use his own occupation or profession for the service of people and mankind.

As an example, this type of success is achieved by political rulers, military leaders, fanatic religious leaders, and other authoritative leaders.

Sets of success criteria can be characterized as a combination of absolute, relative, and personal criteria. The resulting criterion is generally stronger than the two criteria considered separately since it includes distinct components that the individual uses to achieve his success.

The possible sets of success criteria as a result of combination of the different sets are:

- Absolute criteria- Relative criteria
- Absolute criteria- Personal criteria
- Relative criteria- Personal criteria
- Absolute criteria- Relative criteria-Personal criteria

Based on the above success model, it can be concluded that the success criteria combination set

Absolute Criteria- Relative Criteria- Personal Criteria

offers the strictest success characterization, as the criteria include divine laws and commandments, professional impact on people, and the individual's own values, inspiration, interests, and goals to achieve success.

The Elements of Success

The elements of success can be summarized by the different steps taken during a lifetime to achieve and reach success. The elements of success are shown in Exhibit 2 and include

- Focus
- Goals
- Achievements
- Success

The elements of focus include

- Education and knowledge acquired in educational institutions.
- Profession and experience exerted and acquired during one's professional life.
- Character and values that are inherent to the individual or were acquired through family life, religious practice, and peer pressure.
- Judgement and interpretation of facts that are necessary to set and focus on the individual's goals.

Of particular interest among the elements of focus on goals is the combination of education/knowledge and integrity and values that are essential in yielding credibility of individual in trusting oneself in the process of setting the focus and reachability of his goals.

Other external components and factors influence the individual to allow him to set up appropriate goals to make them more realistic and reachable. The external factors are:

- Government factors related to laws, regulations, and political factors that may facilitate or make more difficult the setting and reachability of goals.
- Political factors that provide the proper political environment to support the goals to be set and reached.
- Social factors that reflect the social norms and interest of the community as they influence the setting and attainment of goals.
- Legal factors that include the existing laws and the legal system in place as they impact the goals that are set and the legal path to follow in order to reach them.
- Environmental factors that include economic and financial environment in which the goals are set considering the environmental opportunities and constraints.

Once the short- and long-term goals of the individual have been set, the individual will concentrate on the path forward needed to achieve his goals.

Achievement refers to the accomplishment and realization of one's goals that have been initially set.

Achievement may be partial or total with reference to the goals set. Achievement may also take the form of a small accomplishment with modest results or a triumph with accomplishments exceeding the initial goals.

Acceptance is the next step following achievements that have been reached. It is an important step that usually includes social, political, legal, and economic components.

Social acceptance represents acceptance by the local people where the achievement took place and by other affected people that have benefited from the achievement. The latter form of acceptance implies a universal dimension of the benefits provided by the achievement.

Legal acceptance is a form of acceptance where the achievements have been successful in overcoming legal challenges, thus providing benefits to the people without any form of legal hindrance.

Economic acceptance refers to achievements that have provided clear financial and economic benefits to the people. This form of acceptance is justified by the economic and financial benefits obtained without any form of financial or economic burden on the people.

Political acceptance is probably the most difficult and unpredictable form of acceptance of the achievement. Political acceptance is obtained by lobbying legislators, politicians, and other officials to put in evidence the benefits and shortfalls of the achievements, thus strengthening the political support for the achievements. The political challenge to the benefit of the achievements may be an intense and time-consuming process where the benefits of the achievements may be criticized or questioned. Ultimately, political acceptance of the achievements may be obtained through legislation or may be rejected. Another possible outcome may also be to put limitations or restrictions regarding the benefits provided by the achievements. This will lead to partial political acceptance of the achievements.

It must be noted that the acceptance step to success is time-dependent, and therefore subject to change.

Recognition represents a level higher than acceptance as the goals and achievements reached by the individual have been widely accepted and the accomplishments are fully acknowledged. Recognition represents a form of consecration of acceptance where the different forms of acceptance have been brought to a higher level of reference for the individual. As a result, the individual, through his accomplishments, has reached a high level of consideration among his peers and the public. The individual has become an authority in his field of specialization and, in some cases, has achieved renown and fame.

Recognition therefore allows the individual to reach a form of notoriety where his reputation is at stake: by achieving recognition, the success of a lifetime has been achieved.

The question remains: can you reach success by achieving acceptance without recognition? Is recognition so important as to be the only key to success? The answers to these questions are not easy. Acceptance covers important aspects in the acknowledgment of the achievements of an individual. In particular, it can be shown that in many instances acceptance can easily lead to recognition in the social, legal, and economic domains as evidence of the benefits of the accomplishments are tangible and can be proven, thus leading to recognition. The major difficulty remains in the political domain as political acceptance does not easily and necessarily lead to political recognition. Political acceptance is a form of acceptance that is easier than political recognition. The political benefits acquired by achievements are difficult to quantify and include many "intangible" benefits difficult to demonstrate. In addition, political recognition is a component of success that is time-dependent, usually acquired at a specific time and under specific circumstances. Political acceptance is less time-dependent and more easily acquired than political recognition through tangible accomplishments.

Political recognition is therefore a form of acknowledgment that is very important to success and that is to be made permanent if success must be achieved.

Acceptance is therefore not enough to achieve success at the contemplated level. To do so, acceptance needs full recognition.

Permanent recognition is therefore key to permanent success.

The Levels of Success

5.1 Success Levels

The levels of success achieved during a successful life are important in determining the impact of the individual's life onto his community at a specific time in history. The impact, in general, must be positive with clear benefits to the people affected. The success has to be acknowledged according to relative criteria as the individual's deeds are being accepted and recognized by the people directly concerned. Only in a few cases, absolute criteria may be applied as divine influence or power may have contributed to the individual's success, and thus full recognition by the people.

The levels of success at different levels of intensity are listed in Exhibit 3. This list is not intended to be fully comprehensive or complete but can be used to provide different levels of success that can be achieved depending on the merit of what was accomplished and if and how the success has been accepted and acknowledged.

The list of success levels includes

- Performance where the task or deed has been performed successfully.
- Completion that involves performing the task and carrying it to full completion.
- Fulfillment of the task through performance and successful execution.

- Accomplishment where the objectives of the task have been successfully met or partially exceeded.
- Achievement which is the result of a notable deed of task accomplishment.
- Exploit that involves performing a task or deed successfully accomplished under heroic conditions.
- Triumph where the task has been performed and completed with mastery and success and where all expectations of success have been exceeded.

It should be noted that the above list includes levels of success that may vary with or overlap with other levels. Nevertheless, the list provides reference levels that can be used as a tool to characterize success.

The levels assigned may also vary with time, as temporal circumstances and time may contribute to upgrade or downgrade the level initially assigned. Using success levels to measure a successful life is always possible, as success levels provide a qualitative assessment of the individual's success in life. In addition, these levels become important points of reference and may be included in history.

The following observations may be made with respect to the levels of success achieved.

- Absolute criteria have a great influence on the level of success achieved by the individual.
- Relative and personal criteria have no divine influence or guidance. As a result, these criteria will have a lesser influence on the level of success achieved. The level of success achieved will also be expected to be time sensitive.

5.2 Beyond Success

An important question that arises when one considers the different levels of success is what lies ahead once success has been achieved or, in other words, what remains to be done once the targeted level of success has been reached.

To answer this question, one must understand that the success process is evolutionary and that the individual can keep achieving successes until a certain level is reached. This level is reached once the individual has met absolute, relative, personal criteria, or a combination thereof.

In this situation, the individual's major goal is to stay at the level of success achieved, alleviate the decay of success with time, and maintain his fame as long as possible. This will be performed by any possible means at the disposal of the individual, such as social, legal, economic, financial, spiritual, or political means.

The individual is then expected to reach another level of success or fame until his death. Ultimately, the individual's success level or fame will be assessed by the recognition of his contributions to society, by his legacy, and by history.

5.3 The Role of Money

For some people, money means they will get to buy goods to fulfill their material needs, including food and shelter. For others, money means they will get to enjoy life experiences and adventures. Others may believe that money will bring better opportunities for their families.

Many people, however, will consider the net worth of the individuals as a measure of their self-worth, a clear indication of one's individual success.

The levels of success as defined in Section 5.1 may be assessed in a quantitative way by adding a monetary value to one's life achievements, either for each accomplishment, or for one's life.

The advantages of this approach are the following:

- Using a monetary value is a convenient way to quantify one's success.
- Using money allows to establish a direct relationship between success and its financial impact and recognition by the people affected.
- Using money allows to set a scale to measure the recognition of one's success.

Unfortunately, using a monetary value to assess the success level of an individual's life presents many disadvantages that are:

- Money changes value with time which makes it difficult to quantify success over long periods of time.
- Money cannot quantify success adequately as absolute and relative success criteria are not being completely used.
- Money ignores the effect on success achieved through divine power or human power.
- Money ignores intangible accomplishments due to values, inspiration, initiative, and personal goals.
- Money ignores the effect of lost or wasted time.
- Money cannot quantify any effects related to the individual's health and well-being.
- Money does not account for the width and intensity of recognition of the individual's accomplishments.

For example, the statement that you need to make a lot of money to be successful in life is not accurate and may be misleading. Indeed, money could be considered at most as a tool for financial independence and success. But money fails to bring recognition to the individual who has achieved success through personal values and achievements in areas where money is irrelevant such as in the military, professional, political, or spiritual domains.

Other areas where money cannot bring any form of recognition and success are

- Happiness
- Love
- Health
- Talent
- Values
- Peace

Finally, money is a representative tool that also describes financial stratification with levels ranging from financial stability, security, freedom, and wealth. These monetary levels may not be used accurately by themselves as benchmarks to represent levels of a successful life.

5.4 The Role of Power

The level of success of an individual may be assessed in a qualitative way by considering the power acquired by the individual as a result of his success in a specific achievement or during his whole lifetime.

Absolute power as related to absolute criteria would refer to a divine or absolute influence given to the individual to cause changes and influence others in their behavior. In this respect, power belongs to the leader as he uses his power to shape social groups and followers.

The success of the life of the individual would be assessed by the power of the individual during his lifetime, his achievements, and his legacy that would remain long after the individual's death.

Examples of such absolute power are found mainly in the success of religious, spiritual, and political leaders (such as Jesus Christ, Buddha, Confucius, Vishnu, and other divine individuals, religious saints, and leaders), prophets, kings, and others.

The power of these individuals is mostly due to their social status and/or the political movement and ideology that they created.

The life of such leaders is usually considered successful because of their legacy. Their success is also confirmed by history.

Relative power as related to relative criteria refers to the capacity given to leaders to influence the behavior of their followers in specific areas such as the professional, military, political, and legal areas.

The success of the life of the individuals is assessed by the power required by the individual during his lifetime. Such power is mostly legitimate, expert, or referent power as the individual is accepted or recognized by the members of his organization.

Relative power is mostly due to the social status of the individual, his class due to his economic situation, or his political position.

The life of this individual may be considered successful because of the power he wielded. This power, however, is relatively short-lived, as the individual is no more in a position of power for any reason or may have died.

In this case, the success of the life of the individual is decided by consideration of his contributions to society or his professional legacy.

Personal power as related to personal criteria refers to the personal capacity of leaders to influence the behavior of their followers. These leaders acquired their power because of their achievements using their personal values, inspirations, and personal goals. The power of these leaders is mostly personal, expert, or referent. If acquired by force, this power may not be legitimate or may be coercive.

Personal power is mostly due to social status, class, or personal political desire of the individual.

The life of these individuals may be considered successful because of the power they acquired. This power, however, may be short-lived, as the individual is no longer in a position of power.

The success of the life of these individuals is decided by their political legacy, their contributions to society, or by history.

Cases of Successful and Unsuccesful Life

This section reviews a list of cases of successful and unsuccessful lives as they are described under specific conditions related to the individual's goals, professional situations, and prospective achievements.

This list is only provided for informative and illustrative purposes. It is not intended to be comprehensive and complete. Instead, the list provides current representative cases for review of successful life. Situations that may impact a successful life according to the case reviewed are also discussed.

6.1 A Life of Pleasure

Is a life of pleasure a successful life?

This question was initially raised by the French philosopher Jean-Marie Frey (Ref.4).

The individual is a being incarnated in a physical body. There is a tendency to believe that when we have pleasure, our existence becomes lighter and easier to endure.

It is obvious that humans prefer pleasure to having pain.

Pain may be considered a universal condition, whereas pleasure is not.

Our wisdom consists of lessening the impact of pain so that we can express pleasure. The absence of pain leads to a life of pleasure. But pleasure is not an absolute dimension of human life. It is limited and, thus, cannot exist all by itself. It must be associated with another human component, such as conscience. Pleasure may also be associated with a movement with varying intensity.

Therefore, to achieve success in life, one must have something more than pleasure.

It remains that a successful life is not a life without pleasure. But a successful life is not only a life of pleasure, as the individual becomes tired of pleasure.

A successful life must include pleasure of some sort, but pleasure with conscience. This pleasure, however, is not an absolute dimension of life. Pleasure may be reached as a complement to the individual's achievements and success.

6.2 A Life of Idleness

Is a life of idleness a successful life?

Idleness implies the absence of activity, some kind of laziness that results in no contribution or effort toward a specific goal or achievement.

An idle person is incapable of providing any form of effort focused at a worthwhile goal.

Life spent in idleness ignores all the elements of success, either with respect to absolute or relative criteria, with a view to accomplishing any task worthwhile of an achievement toward the benefit of people or mankind.

Idleness leads to selfish goals and behavior since this characteristic concentrates on one's self without any other purpose and accomplishment.

Life under such conditions does not show any positive elements for success and, therefore, cannot be successful.

6.3 Life of Leisure

Is a life of leisure a successful life?

Leisure implies the freedom that the individual enjoys by the cessation of work activity. A life of leisure would therefore refer to a lifetime free from work and duties, resulting in no contribution or effort toward a specific goal or achievement.

An individual of leisure is totally concentrated on preserving his or her freedom from any kind of work, thereby never being able to provide any form of effort focused on a worthwhile goal.

Life spent on leisure is usually spent out of selfishness and concentrates on the need for immediate personal satisfaction.

A life of leisure ignores all the elements of success with respect to either absolute or relative criteria with a view to accomplishing any task worthwhile for the benefit of anybody, except the individual himself.

Life in this form of self-reward and immediate satisfaction resulting from leisure cannot be successful.

6.4 A Life of Privileges

Is a life of privileges a successful life?

Privileges imply a right or immunity granted as a benefit or advantage to an individual that results in an effort or a contribution toward a specific goal or achievement with a clear acceptance or acknowledgment. Regardless of the level of effort made by the individual, the effort performed will be recognized as a success.

A privileged individual will provide some form of effort focused on a worthwhile goal. However, most of the elements of success are expected to be bypassed because of the privileges initially granted to the individual.

Success may therefore be achieved without talent or merit regardless of the outcome of the task performed.

In most cases, privilege leads to easily achievable goals and predictable outcomes, since it concentrates on oneself regardless of the level of accomplishment performed.

Life under privileged conditions will be successful in most cases as the achievements of the privileged individual, as modest as they may be, will be acknowledged.

Life is expected to be even more successful if the individual uses his values and all his resources to focus on his achievements and success.

Situations may occur, however, when the individual possesses too few elements for success, loses focus on his goals, and does not achieve success, regardless of the privileges initially granted to him.

6.5 A Life of Work and Dedication

Is a life of work and dedication a successful life?

Such a life is the most common type of life that is offered and programmed by modern societies. The individuals are expected to work to earn money that, in turn, is used to buy their material needs and allow them to become financially secure.

As financial security is achieved, such a life offers the opportunity for everyone to excel in his or her profession.

The major elements of success that include goals and achievements are mostly due to relative criteria of individual professionalism at the service of society and mankind.

In general, a life of work and dedication results in fulfillment of goals and achievements set by the individual. The individual succeeds in being a professional to serve society.

The level of success of the individual, however, may be limited unless the individual, through work and dedication, has been accepted and recognized as an expert in the field.

No matter how talented and skilled the individual is, the individual will not achieve a level of success higher than fulfillment or accomplishments if he is not accepted and acknowledged by his management. The lack of acceptance and recognition may be due to various reasons such as lack of support from the management of the organization, lack of political support, etc.

Due to lack of acceptance and recognition, the individual may retire from professional life as an "unrecognized talent" that success has eluded. Deep inside himself, however, such an individual may believe that he has achieved success by fulfilling his professional goals.

6.6 A Life of Isolation

Is a life of isolation a successful life?

A life of isolation involves a life where the individual does not mix or interact with other people or with society. The individual earns a living by being an independent professional providing services to society without seeking any form of acceptance or recognition. For this individual, there are no relative criteria of success such as wielding military, political, legal, or spiritual power. The individual has chosen to live and serve society by being isolated from others. The criteria for success of this individual are therefore mostly personal and are based on values, inspiration, and self-interest. The success criteria for such an individual may also have an absolute component such as religious faith and divine inspiration, although isolation by itself does not represent an absolute criterion.

The level of success achieved by an isolated individual may be high, as he may reach a personal interpretation of life and its meaning, including personal recognition and success. Acceptance and recognition may also come from society later. However, through isolation, the individual does not seek any form of acceptance or recognition during his lifetime.

A life of isolation may therefore be successful as judged and interpreted by the individual himself. Such a life, however, may not meet the relative success criteria set by society.

6.7 A Life of Prayer and Meditation

Is a life of prayer and meditation a successful life?

A life of prayer and meditation is characterized by an individual (or a group of individuals) dedicated to praying to God and meditating to fulfill religious aspirations and needs. The criteria of success in life for this type of individual are mostly absolute, as the prayer invokes God and is recited according to prescribed texts and rituals that must be followed. Prayer and meditation represent a form of direct communication with God, as if they are inspired and influenced by a divine power. Such a life is also expected to be lived according to strict divine laws and commandments.

Personal success criteria may also be applied to this kind of life as the individual will seek to fulfill divine requirements aligned with his personal values, focus, and interests.

In general, an individual who has devoted his life to prayer and meditation will not seek any form of acceptance or recognition by others, except by his peers and others with the same faith and similar life requirements.

Relative criteria may also apply to this kind of life, as a life of prayer and meditation may be used to influence the lives of others by providing religious and spiritual guidance. In some cases, such a life may be imposed onto others through religious authority and political power, despite legal constraints of separation of church and state.

A life of prayer and meditation may be quite successful as lived and interpreted by the individual since, first and foremost, such a life is lived according to divine laws and commandments.

Such a life, however, may not be successful if the individual loses focus, deviates from the set religious goals, or abandons his faith.

Situations that May Impact a Successful Life of Prayer and Meditation:

- The individual loses focus and faith to continue or persevere in a life of prayer and meditation
- The individual deviates from the religious commandments and laws of his faith
- The individual has lost his integrity and credibility
- The individual is not recognized by his religious institution

6.8 A Life of Travel and Discovery (T&D)

Is a life of travel and discovery a successful life?

A life of travel and discovery is characterized by the life of an individual dedicated to travel the world and make discoveries of natural and archaeological sites. The individual may be an explorer or an archaeologist eager to discover new sites that may be the remnants of old or extinct civilizations.

After much work and time, the level of success achieved by the individual is usually very high and is mostly obtained because of relative criteria directed at promoting and developing further the knowledge and understanding of the world and civilizations.

Personal criteria for success may also be applied by the individual as he seeks to achieve his goals guided by his personal values, judgment, and self-interest.

Since the endeavor of the individual has a lot of visibility, acceptance and recognition of the work will be essential and actively sought.

The life of this type of individual will be successful if the results of his travels and discoveries are meaningful and significant, and if his work is fully acknowledged and recognized. This individual may not achieve success if he loses focus and does not reach his goals because of difficulties and uncertainties in his work and his findings.

Situations that May Impact a Successful Life of Travel and Discovery (T&D):

- The individual loses focus of his T&D mission
- The goals of the T&D mission become elusive and difficult to reach due to unexpected uncertainties
- The T&D does not get the visibility and recognition it expects
- Lack of financial support for the T&D mission

6.9 A Life of Arts

Is a life of art a successful life?

A life of arts is characterized by an individual dedicated to being an artist in the vast domain of arts, such as music, painting, literature, sculpture, visual arts, movie acting or directing, etc.

Since the work and performance of the individual have a lot of visibility, acceptance and recognition of the artist's work is essential to the artist's success. After many years of being unknown, the artist may achieve success at a very high level (such as triumph) through high recognition and fame.

The artist's success is recognized through relative criteria as the artist, through his work and performance, is dedicated to his work and seeks to satisfy the public.

Personal criteria are dominant, however, as the artist will undoubtedly include in his work personal values, beliefs, and inspiration directed at his very personal goals to achieve success.

The life of the artist will generally be successful if his work and performance are fully acknowledged and recognized by his peers, his critics, and the public.

There are situations, however, when the artist will not be successful during his lifetime, such as lack of recognition, lack of visibility, or obsolescence. In this case, the artist will never reach his goals and become famous. Recognition and fame may occur after the artist's death.

Situations that May Impact a Successful Life of Arts:

- The artist lacks visibility
- The success of the artist is elusive

— The art of the artist is not understood or is obsolete
— The work of the artist is not recognized

6.10 A Biological Life

Is a biological life a successful life?

A biological life refers to a life where the individual lives a totally independent life where social norms and interactions are absent. The individual lives a life of survival and biological existence without any form of integration into society. The individual does not interact with anyone and has no faith expressed in the form of religious belief. The individual lives essentially through his instincts of survival to satisfy his existential needs. The individual believes in the survival of the fittest and spends his entire life in a purely physical and biological environment.

There are no absolute or relative criteria to be applied to assess the success of such a life. The goals of this life are essentially related to biological existence and survival in a purely natural environment. The individual is isolated from society by choice and does not seek any form of acceptance or recognition by others.

Most of the elements of success of such a life are absent.

The only form of success of such a life can be assessed by longevity of life as the individual strives to live and survive by instinct in his natural environment.

A purely biological life therefore may not be successful as judged by absolute or relative criteria. Personal success criteria are absent as well. There are no measurable levels of success in such a life.

6.11 The Life of the Rich

Can the life of the rich be a successful life?

The lives of the rich are dependent on the money and wealth that the rich possess. For the rich, goals and achievement are intimately related and mostly dependent on what money can buy.

In general, absolute criteria of success do not apply to the rich as limitless space and time cannot be controlled by money. Relative criteria, however, do apply to the rich's successful lives, as money is widely used to set focus and goals on relative projects that may benefit individuals and people, but mostly to allow the rich to become richer. The financial and economic criteria to measure the rich's life success are therefore the reflection of the self-networth that the rich were able to achieve during their lifetime.

Personal criteria, based on the individual's character and values, although not directly dependent on wealth, may also be applied to assess the rich's life success.

Acceptance and recognition of the rich are mostly based on wealth and financial net worth. Other forms of recognition based on merit and contributions to society and mankind are not directly sought after by the rich, except for charitable causes.

Therefore, the lives of the rich and wealthy may or may not be successful, as the criteria to make this determination are mostly dependent on the financial impact made by the rich on society.

The lives of the rich will therefore be successful if the rich make a positive financial impact with focus and goals achieved and directed to the benefit of society.

The rich individual will not be successful in life if he makes a negative financial impact on society or if his money is misused, wasted, or used against the interest of society. More money earned by the rich does not necessarily mean more success in the rich's lives.

Situations that May Impact a Successful Life of the Rich:

- The rich do not have the proper knowledge and character to make a positive financial impact on society
- The rich show poor judgment in allocating their financial support
- The rich's integrity is questioned and their financial support must be discontinued
- The financial support of the rich is not recognized

6.12 The Life of the Poor

Can the life of the poor be a successful life?

In general, the lives of the poor are not dependent on absolute criteria. In some cases, however, devotion and dedication from charitable individuals can be associated with divine power used for the benefit of society and mankind.

Relative criteria are the dominant criteria of the poor life's success as the individual will strive by his work to be a social and/or spiritual leader dedicated to society and mankind for a charitable cause.

Personal criteria based on the individual's character, values, and level of dedication, regardless of his poverty level, may also be used to determine the poor life's success.

The poor are expected to emphasize the positive elements of their success, including their integrity, judgment, and society-oriented goals. Through his achievements the poor individual will strive to gain acceptance and recognition for his work and dedication. For this individual, recognition will be key to achieving a successful life.

In some situations, the poor may get rid of their poverty as they finds success. But, nevertheless, they are mostly expected to persist in their benevolent endeavors.

The lives of the poor may not be successful if they lose focus of their goals and are not persistent in their endeavors, or if their lives are wasted by creating a negative impact on society.

Situations that May Impact a Successful Life of the Poor:

- The poor lack focus and persistence to reach their goals
- The poor lack financial and political support
- The poor lack the knowledge, character, and integrity to achieve success

6.13 The Life of the Military

Can the life of the military be a successful life?

Absolute criteria are in general not applicable to a military individual as absolute elements of success such as eternity and infinity do not apply. In very few cases, however, history has shown that military success may have absolute elements, as it is associated with religious beliefs, goals, or divine commandments.

Relative criteria are also important as they relate to the military professional who serve their country and who are socially responsible for defending the national territory, the people, and freedom. The military must also be ethical and respectful in all their duties and endeavors. It is essential for the military to have high morality and ethical behavior.

Personal criteria based on the military professional's character, values, and goals are essential to the military's life success.

Based on the above criteria, the life of the military individual may or may not be successful.

The life of the military individual will be successful if his life is spent as it was intended, i.e., serving his country with pride, honor, and ethics.

The military individual's life will not be successful if his life is wasted on the battlefield, devoted to the wrong cause, or used against the people the military is supposed to serve and protect.

Acceptance and recognition of the military is based on merit, dedication to the country, and continual service. During challenging times such as wars and internal unrest, military leaders are in general highly recognized.

Situations that May Impact a Successful Life of the Military:

- The military professional is devoting his military life to the wrong cause
- The military professional is involved with military action against his own people
- The military professional fails to reach a position of leadership due to poor character and values
- The military professional is not recognized by his superiors

6.14 The Life of the Politician

Can the life of the politician be a successful life?

The life of the politician is mostly determined by how relative and personal criteria are effectively used to serve the elected politician. Absolute criteria are rarely used by politicians, as political success is generally not due to absolute elements. In rare instances, however, politicians use religious concepts and goals to be elected to exert political power linked to religious parties or groups.

Relative criteria are important as they relate to the political officials who are elected to serve their country. These politicians are socially responsible to make political decisions in the best interest of the people who elected them.

Personal criteria are applicable to politicians as they seek to get elected based on their characters, personal values, and focus on goals that are consistent with their personal beliefs.

In general, the life of the politician will be successful if the relative and personal criteria are met. The politician will then achieve acceptance and recognition by the people. He will achieve success in his political career. Ultimately, the success of the politician is decided by the voters during his lifetime. In the long-term, however, the success of the politician is decided by his legacy.

The life of the politician will not be successful and thus will be shortened if he loses sight of what he was elected for, therefore losing the trust and confidence of the people he was elected to represent and serve.

The life of the politician will not be successful if the politician misused or abused his power, lost credibility, or made decisions which are not in the best interest of his constituents. In particular, the politician's career will be shortened if he puts his interests ahead of the interests of his constituents.

Situations that May Impact a Successful Life of the Politician:

- The politician misused or abused his power
- The politician lost his credibility with his constituents
- The politician's integrity and character are compromised
- The politician addresses and supports issues that are not aligned with his constituents' best interest

6.15 The Life of the Doctor

Can the life of the doctor be a successful life?

The life of the doctor is determined by the success of the relative and personal criteria as they are applied to the doctor's professional life. Absolute criteria are not used in evaluating the success of the doctor's life.

Relative criteria are the most important criteria for success when they are applied to the professional dedication and skills of the doctor as he cares for his patients.

Personal criteria are used to assess the doctor's life success. These criteria consist mainly of the doctor's character, personal values, professional focus, judgment, and credibility.

The life of the doctor will be successful if the doctor's relative and personal criteria are satisfied. The doctor will then achieve his professional goals and reach success through acceptance and recognition as an expert in his discipline. Ultimately, the success of the doctor is decided by recognition among his peers and by referral of his patients.

The life of the doctor will not be successful if the doctor does not satisfy the medical needs of his patients by providing his best professional services, if he loses his professional focus, or if he is not properly recognized by his peers or the medical community.

Situations that May Impact a Successful Life of the Doctor:

- The doctor breaks his Hippocratic Oath for his personal interest such as for money or profit
- The doctor breaks his Hippocratic Oath by willingly prescribing the wrong treatment against the patients' interest
- The doctor breaks his Hippocratic Oath by causing harm or hurt to the patient

6.16 The Life of the Fashion Model

Can the life of the fashion model be a successful life?

The life of the fashion model is determined by the success of the relative and personal criteria as they are applied to the model's professional life. Absolute criteria are not used in assessing the success of the model's life.

Relative criteria are important success criteria as they relate to the professional skills and know-how of the fashion model when she dedicates herself to wearing and exhibiting clothes that have been especially designed for ongoing fashion trends.

Personal criteria are used to assess the model's life success. These criteria include mainly the physical traits of the model, the character and personality that she projects, and the professional focus and dedication that she brings to fashion display and exhibition.

The life of the fashion model will be successful if the model's relative and personal criteria are met. The model will then reach her professional goals and achieve success through acceptance and recognition as a supermodel by the fashion professionals and the public.

The professional life of the fashion model will not be successful and will be brief if the model does not maintain her physical traits and appearance or she loses her focus and dedication to fashion design and exhibition.

Situations that May Impact a Successful Life of the Fashion Model:

- The fashion model loses focus on her basic task related to fashion design and exhibition
- The fashion model does not maintain the physical appearance for exhibiting design fashion
- The fashion model does not adapt to new fashion trends
- The fashion model does not keep up with competing models

6.17 The Life of the Attorney

Can the life of the attorney be a successful life?

The life of the attorney is determined by the success of the relative and personal criteria as they are applied to the attorney professional's life. Absolute criteria are not used in assessing the success of the attorney's life, as infinite dimension of space and time and legal absolutes are not applicable.

Relative criteria are the most characteristic criteria for success as they relate to the legal expertise and skills of the attorney as he represents and pleads for his clients or is a magistrate in court.

Personal criteria are used to assess the attorney's life success. These criteria consist mostly of the attorney's character, personal values, communication skills, and most of all, his professional focus, integrity, and credibility. These personal traits are essential to the success of the attorney, as he evolves as a legal expert, a legislator, or a magistrate.

The life of the attorney will be successful if the attorney's relative and personal success criteria are met. The attorney will then achieve his professional goals and success through acceptance and recognition as a legal expert. Ultimately, the success of the attorney is decided by his recognition among his peers, referral from his clients, and his work performance as a legislator, an elected official, or a magistrate.

The life of the attorney will not be successful if

- The attorney does not do his utmost for his clients as a lawyer
- The attorney does not adequately represent his constituents as a legislator
- Does not perform effectively as a magistrate

Situations that May Impact a Successful Life of the Attorney:

- The attorney's relationship with his clients is compromised
- The attorney's credibility, judgment, or integrity are questioned
- The attorney is not adequately recognized by his peers or other legal experts
- The attorney cannot perform effectively as a legislator, an elected official, or a magistrate

6.18 The Life of the Engineer/Scientist

Can the life of the engineer/scientist be a successful life?

The life of the engineer/scientist is determined by the success of the relative and personal criteria as they are applied to the engineer/scientist's life.

Absolute criteria are not used in assessing the success of the engineer/scientist's life, as infinite dimensions of space and time are not applicable to the rational approach traditionally used in the field of engineering and science. Scientific absolutes, such as natural phenomena and absolute scientific laws and principles, are not in the scope of success assessment and thus will not be considered.

Relative criteria are the most applicable criteria for assessing success as they relate to the knowledge, expertise, and skills of the engineer/scientist as he strives to use scientific principles to solve engineering and science problems to the benefit of people and mankind. This type of criteria is perhaps one of the most important to the engineer/scientist profession as engineering and science are being used by experts to the benefit of others using all the scientific disciplines.

Personal criteria are used to assess the engineer/scientist's life success. These criteria consist mostly of the engineer/scientist's character, personal values and, most of all, professional focus, integrity, and credibility.

These personal traits are essential to the success of the engineer/scientist as he evolves as an engineering expert, a dedicated scientist, or an eminent scientific and professional authority.

The life of the engineer/scientist will be successful if the engineer/scientist's relative and personal success criteria are satisfied. The engineer/scientist will then achieve his personal goals and achieve success through acceptance and recognition as an engineer/scientist expert. Ultimately, the success of an engineer/scientist is decided by recognition among his peers, his management, and his students.

The life of the engineer/scientist will not be successful if the engineer/scientist is not recognized by his peers or his management as an expert in the field. In the absence of such a recognition, the engineer/scientist may seek and achieve recognition from the engineering/science community as an individual contributor.

Situations that May Impact a Successful Life of the Engineer/Scientist:

– The Engineer/Scientist knowingly makes technical decisions that are against the interest of the project or that are unethical
– The Engineer/Scientist knowingly makes technical decisions that are massively destructive against mankind
– The Engineer/Scientist knowingly withholds or does not disclose technical facts that are unsafe or have dire consequences against mankind

6.19 The Life of the Teacher

Can the life of the teacher be a successful life?

The life of the teacher is determined by the success of the relative and personal criteria as they are applied to the teacher's professional life. Absolute criteria are not used in evaluating the success of the teacher's life as absolute educational criteria related to absolute dimensions and divine influence are generally not applicable. The only exception is religious teaching performed and administered in parochial schools.

Relative criteria are the most relevant criteria for success as they relate to the educational expertise and skills of the teacher in his endeavor of teaching and educating his students.

Personal criteria may be used to some extent to assess the teacher's life success. These criteria consist mostly of the teacher's character, personal values, and, most of all, focus, credibility, and inspirational role for his students. These personal traits are essential to the success of the teacher as he interacts and leaves a lasting impact on his students.

The life of the teacher will be successful if the teacher's relative and personal success criteria are satisfied. The teacher will then reach his professional goals and achieve success through recognition as an educational expert in his field. Ultimately, the success of a teacher is decided by recognition among his peers, his school management, and his students. The teacher may also publish educational and pedagogical material for his students. In this manner, the teacher may be recognized by the public at a national or international level.

The life of the teacher will not be successful, however, if he loses focus of his teaching and dedication to his students and if he is not recognized by the school management or by his peers as an educational expert.

Situations that May Impact a Successful Life of the Teacher:

- The teacher does not keep up with changes in education
- The teacher is not accountable to peers or students
- The teacher does not improve teaching methods or students' guidance methods
- The teacher is reluctant to be a role model for his students

6.20 The Life of the Nurse

Can the life of the nurse be a successful life?

The life of the nurse is determined by the success of the relative and personal criteria as they are applied to the nurse's professional life. Absolute criteria are not used in evaluating the success of the nurse's life.

Relative criteria are the most relevant criteria for success as they relate to the expertise and skills of the nurse in her practice of nursing with doctors and patients.

Personal criteria may be used within limits to assess the nurse's life success. These criteria consist mostly of the nurse's character, personal values, and professional focus and dedication. These traits are essential to the success of the nurse as she interacts and leaves a caring and lasting impression on the doctors she reports to and, most importantly, on the patients she cares for.

The life of the nurse will be successful if the nurse's relative and personal success criteria are met. The nurse will then reach her professional goals and achieve success through recognition as a nursing expert. Ultimately, the success of the nurse is decided by her recognition among her peers, the medical and administrative staff, and the patients she cares for.

The nurse may also achieve further professional success by acquiring advanced nursing credentials to become a nurse practitioner.

The life of the nurse will not be successful, however, if the nurse loses her professional focus and interest in her work or if she is involved in neglect or abuse of patients. In this case, she will not be recognized by her peers and by the medical and administrative staff.

Situations that May Impact a Successful Life of the Nurse:

- – The nurse loses interest in interacting with patients and doctors
- – The nurse does not strictly follow doctor's order
- – The nurse does not show compassion towards patients

6.21 The Life of the Minister

Can the life of the minister be a successful life?

The life of the minister is based on strong personal criteria that include the character, devotion, values, and goals that are representative of a religious leader. These traits, however, are subject to strict compliance with religious requirements and beliefs derived from divine laws and commandments.

Relative criteria are important criteria as they relate to religious leaders and ministers who serve the spiritual needs of their congregations and who are socially responsible to make religious decisions in accordance with religious principles. The relative criteria also relate to the religious knowledge and skills of the ministers in their role of leading and inspiring their followers.

Absolute criteria are important criteria in assessing the minister's life success as religious absolute dimensions of space and time, as well as reference to divine revelations and supernatural phenomena guide the minister's life in accordance with his religious beliefs and endeavor.

The life of the minister will be successful if the minister's absolute, relative, and personal success criteria are satisfied. The minister will then reach his professional and spiritual goals and achieve success through acceptance and recognition as a religious leader.

Ultimately, the success of a minister is decided by his recognition among his peers, his followers, and the religious authority of his ministry.

The life of the minister will not be successful if

- He loses focus of his duty and does not serve adequately the spiritual needs of his community
- He is not recognized as a religious leader by his followers, his peers, or the religious authority of his ministry
- He abandons his religious principles and faith

Situations that May Impact a Successful Life of the Minister:

- The minister loses credibility with his followers
- The minister deviates from religious principles and faith
- The minister misuses or abuses his authority with his followers
- The minister cannot effectively assume his leadership role

6.22 The Life of the Mother

Can the life of the mother be a successful life?

The life of the mother is determined by the success of the relative and personal criteria as they are applied to the mother's family life.

Absolute criteria are not used in assessing the success of the mother's life, as motherhood is not an absolute criterion per se and divine influence is not applicable.

Relative and personal criteria are the most relevant criteria for success as they relate to the mother character, personal and family values, and most of all integrity, judgment, and credibility in the mother's role in the family. These personal traits are essential to the success of the mother as she gives birth, raises, and interacts with her children and makes a lasting inspirational and motivational impact on her children.

These criteria will also help the mother focus on her goals and achieve success by raising her children in a family environment conducive of values, integrity, and love. By her central role in the family, the mother will be accepted, respected, and recognized by her family and, most importantly, by her children.

The mother is also expected to be devoted to her spouse. Ultimately, the success of the mother is decided by the success of her husband and, more particularly, the success of her own children as they evolve in life using the values and principles inculcated to them by their mother. The righteous mother is expected to always be respected and loved by her children and by her family. Acceptance and recognition of the mother will always be provided by her children and husband as a part of family principles.

The life of the mother will not be totally successful, however, if her marriage is compromised in any way, or if she is divorced. In this case, raising her children will become a more challenging task.

A mother will not be successful if she neglects to accomplish her role as a mother, or worse, if she abandons her spouse or her children. In this case, she will hurt her family, and, more particularly, her children.

Situations that May Impact a Successful Life of the Mother:

- The mother is unfaithful to her spouse and her family
- The mother neglects, abuses, or abandons her children and spouse
- The mother fails to be a role model to and instill values and principles in her children
- Ther mother fails to provide material needs for her children
- The mother seeks to divorce and threatens the integrity of her family

6.23 The Life of the Father

Can the life of the father be a successful life?

The life of the father is determined by the success of the relative and personal criteria as they are applied to the father's family life.

Absolute criteria are not used in assessing the success of the father's life as fatherhood is not an absolute criterion per se, and divine influence is not applicable.

Relative and personal criteria are the most relevant criteria for success as they relate to the skills of the father in his endeavor for educating his children and being a role model.

Personal criteria relate to the father's character, personal and family values, integrity, credibility, and a role model for his children. These personal traits are essential to the success of the father as he raises and interacts with his children and leaves a lasting positive impact on his children.

These criteria will also help the father focus on his goals and achieve success by raising his children in a family environment conducive of values, integrity, and trust. By his essential role in the family, the father is expected to be accepted, respected, and recognized by his spouse and his children.

The father is also expected to be devoted to his wife and children. Ultimately, the success of the father is decided by the success of his own children as they evolve in life using the values and principles inculcated to them by their father. The righteous father is expected to always be respected and loved by his children and by the family he helped found and raise. Acceptance and recognition will always be provided by his children and spouse through family values and ties.

The life of the father will not be totally successful, however, if his marriage is compromised or if he is divorced. In this case, the father's task of raising his children is expected to be more challenging.

A father will not be successful if he loses focus on his family or if he neglects his role as father of the family. The father will fail even further if he is not faithful to his spouse, if he neglects or abuses his children, or worse, if he abandons his spouse and children. In this case, he will hurt his family and, particularly, his children.

Situations that May Impact a Successful Life of the Father:

- The father is unfaithful to his spouse and his family
- The father neglects, abuses, or abandons his children and spouse
- The father fails to be a role model to and instill values in his children
- The father fails to provide material needs for his children
- The father seeks to divorce and threatens the integrity of his family

6.24 The Life of the Farmer

Can the life of the farmer be a successful life?

The life of the farmer is determined by the success of the relative and personal criteria as they are applied to the farmer's life. Absolute criteria are not used in evaluating the success of the farmer's life, as criteria related to absolute dimensions of space and time and divine influence are not applicable.

Relative criteria are the most relevant criteria for success as they relate to the farming expertise and skills of the farmer in his endeavor of carrying out farming tasks and duties for his farm and performing all the associated farm work.

Personal criteria may be used to some extent to assess the farmer's life success. These criteria consist mostly of the farmer's character, personal values, and, most of all, focus, dedication to the farm's work, and resilience. These personal traits are essential to the success of the farmer as he performs farming tasks that may range from cultivating agricultural products, caring for his cattle, or providing the proper irrigation for his land. The farmer must also have business skills for understanding agricultural product markets and negotiating contracts.

The life of the farmer will be successful if the farmer's relative and personal success criteria are satisfied. The farmer will then reach his professional goals and achieve success through recognition as a farming expert in his agricultural field. Ultimately, the success of a farmer is decided by his recognition among fellow farmers and agricultural experts. The farmer's job, however, remains a job that requires hard work, stamina, and resilience for solving operational challenges that include uncertainty, such as the effects of the weather on yearly crops and agricultural markets.

The life of the farmer will not be successful, however, if he loses focus of his farming and agricultural duties, his dedication to his farm and cattle, and understanding and proper handling of all financial farming profitability matters.

Situations that May Impact a Successful Life of the Farmer:

- The farmer loses focus in farming and agricultural duties
- The farmer fails to apply modern technology for farming and raising cattle
- The farmer does not develop business and financial skills for farming profitability

6.25 The Life of the Pilot

Can the life of the pilot be a successful life?

The life of the pilot is determined by the success of the relative and personal criteria as they are applied to the pilot's life. Absolute criteria are not used in evaluating the success of the pilot's life.

Relative criteria are the most relevant criteria for success as they relate to the air navigation expertise and skills of the pilot in his duties and endeavors for flying aircraft for commercial airlines or military operations.

Personal criteria may be used to some extent to assess the pilot's life success. These criteria consist mostly of the pilot's character, personal values, and, most of all, focus, physical and mental stamina, and resilience related to long hours needed for aircraft operations. These personal traits are essential to the success of the pilot as he performs his tasks of flying commercial or military aircraft.

The life of the pilot will be successful if the pilot's relative and personal success criteria are satisfied. The pilot will then achieve his professional goals and achieve success through recognition as a flying expert in his field. Ultimately, the success of a pilot is decided by his recognition among his peers and his company management or military unit command. The pilot faces an additional challenge as he must be physically and mentally ready for his flying mission under all circumstances that may include uncertainties due to technical problems or weather-related difficulties.

The life of the pilot will not be successful, however, if he loses focus of his flying duties and responsibilities, if he does not overcome physical or mental pressure related to flying commercial or military operations, or he is not recognized by his company management or the command of his military unit.

Situations that May Impact a Successful Life of the Pilot:

- The pilot loses focus on his flying duties and responsibilities
- The pilot cannot overcome physical or mental pressure for flying civil or military aircraft
- The pilot is not recognized among peers, company managers, or military commanders

Thoughts for Leading a Successful Life

Leading a successful life is the goal of many individuals who go through life without any precise direction or roadmap but strive to achieve goals of accomplishments, recognition, and success in many aspects of their lives. For these individuals, success is to be reached in one or several areas such as the professional, family, and community areas.

First and foremost, the individual must acquire and possess a basic education with emphasis on knowledge, skills and competence, work ethics, values, and other factors that will allow a clear dedication to work to earn a living for himself, for his family, for society, and for mankind. This education must be applied to lead a professional life with specific goals and achievements over periods of time when the individual will contribute to the needs of society.

The level of success reached in one's professional life must be clearly and regularly assessed and adjusted to continually benefit the individual and society. The level of success can be determined in several ways ranging from personal satisfaction to monetary benefits or to social acceptance and recognition. The latter form of success, recognition, may not be reached during the lifetime of the individual or ever. Nevertheless, the individual should continue and persevere in his endeavor and deliver the expected professional services. The individual should overcome the negative feelings and frustration that come with rejection and the absence of recognition.

The success of the individual will also be assessed according to the absolute, relative, and personal criteria that apply to the individual. For instance, the absolute criteria apply to the divine belief of or influence on the individual. Relative criteria may be in the professional, political, financial, legal, or spiritual domains. Personal criteria may be related to the personal beliefs, values, and goals cherished by the individual.

Second, the individual should concentrate his efforts to set up goals to the benefit of people and achieve those goals with focus, passion, and dedication without specifically expecting immediate benefits or recognition in return.

Specific and important considerations for goals and successful achievements include:

- Goals should be clear, specific, and prioritized
- A detailed plan should be developed to accomplish the goals
- Appropriate and timely action should be taken to achieve the goals with commitment and faith
- Flexibility in strategy should be exercised to adapt to change
- The individual must show creativity and originality
- The individual must have self-confidence and self-esteem
- The individual must show perseverance
- The individual should choose courage over comfort and hard work over complacency
- The individual should always be prepared
- If needed, the individual should take calculated risks
- If needed, the individual should build professional relationships

The following personal character traits must be adopted, developed, and used all along the road to success:

- Curiousness or the deep desire to know
- Concentration that is used to understand and solve problems
- The ability to criticize oneself and draw conclusions of one's performance

Third, leading a successful family life is important to the mental and moral balance of the individual who is struggling in life. Therefore, the individual must strive to succeed with his family, ensuring a stable and supporting family environment.

Impact of AI on A Successful Life

This section reviews and discusses some of the aspects of a new science, Artificial Intelligence (AI), and its expected impact on a successful life whose model was presented in the preceding chapters.

Why AI?

AI is a computer-based science that allows computers to use algorithms and data to simulate human thoughts, reasoning, and processes such as (Ref. 8):

- Reasoning and problem solving
- Knowledge
- Planning
- Learning
- Language-processing
- Perception

Some of the tools currently used by AI are

- Optimization
- Logic
- Probabilistic methods
- Neural networks
- Deep learning
- Specialized languages

Examples of current applications of AI include

- Speech recognition
- Customer services
- Computer/ digital vision
- Recommendation engines
- Finance digitalization

8.1 Impact of AI on Success Criteria

Absolute Success Criteria:

AI is expected to have very little effect on absolute success criteria since AI does not apply infinite limits of time and space in its processing of knowledge and learning. AI uses rational algorithms and thus does not use any absolute qualities of perfection or supernatural phenomena in its functional processes.

Relative Success Criteria:

These success criteria are expected to be mostly affected by AI, as relative criteria of limited time and dimensions, and criteria directly applied to humans are affected. In particular,

- AI is extensively used in military warfare, decision-making, risk-analysis, and "what if" situations
- AI is being used in professional applications where professional functions and management decisions are simulated and optimized. This applies to many professions including financial, legal, business, technology, and government-based functions
- Spiritual power is not expected to be affected by AI

Personal Success Criteria:

It is not known at present to what extent AI is expected to impact personal criteria. Indeed, a priori, AI is not expected to impact significantly personal criteria since these criteria are based on personal traits of character, qualities, values, and personal focus and goals set by the individual. However, using simulation and data analysis, AI may be used to alter the criteria for success set by the individual. In particular, AI may provide selected facts, analyze proprietary data, refer to previous experience, or provide judgment and interpretation on specific issues to influence the individual personal criteria, so that his personal criteria become more aligned with the AI success criteria.

As an example, AI may alter the personal criteria of success in the areas of curiousness, creativity, self-control, persistence, and other personal traits of the individual.

AI may also negatively impact the ethical behavior of the individual (Ref. 3).

Combination of Success Criteria:

AI is expected to impact the criteria made up mostly of relative criteria and personal criteria defined as the set "relative-personal". This set offers an important success characterization where AI can affect the criteria with professional impact on people and the individual's character, personal values, and goals to achieve success.

The resulting criteria are expected to be AI-based criteria designed, operated, and controlled by AI.

At this time, it is not clear to what extent the individual's goals may be impacted by AI, but it is obvious that AI may have the capability to develop the individual's goals for success using powerful computers, algorithms, and databases. The impact of AI may be positive, as it is in agreement with the individual's interests, or negative, as the individual's goals may be modified or substituted to better accommodate and represent AI's interests.

8.2 Impact of AI on Elements of Success

Focus:

Focus may be impacted by AI through the effect of AI on

- Education and knowledge by educating the individual to understand and develop the interests of AI
- Professional experience represented by professional experts
- Character and values of the individual
- Integrity where the individual's integrity is put into question and altered to better fit AI's interests
- Judgment of the individual that may be questioned or biased in favor of AI
- Interpretation of the facts by the individual to better reflect AI's interests

Factors:

The factors that may be mostly impacted by AI are:

- Political factors that provide the proper political environment to support goals to be reached that are more aligned with AI's interests
- Social factors that can be modified to define social norms and community interests that support goals more conforming with AI's interests
- Environmental factors that include economic and financial support in line with AI's interests
- Government factors related to laws and regulations that are aligned with AI's interests
- Legal factors that use the legal system of laws regulating AI

Goals:

The goals of the individual are particularly vulnerable to AI since the elements of success for making up his decision may be altered by AI. In particular, the affected aspects of his short-term and long-term goals are:

- Knowledge that may be superior to the individual's knowledge
- Professional experience
- Factors that are targeted by AI to persuade the individual
- Values such as concentration and persistence
- Judgment that relies on deeper analysis and persuasion

As an example, the individual who needs a washing machine for his short-term home appliance needs may end up being persuaded by AI to buy a stereophonic musical system based on his personal taste and choice.

Similarly, the individual who needs means of transportation may end up buying a new car instead of a used car due to his preferential transportation needs "supposedly determined by AI."

Achievements:

The achievements of the individual may be impacted by AI as the measure of achievements and, hence, the success of the individual is highly recognized by AI since his achievements are aligned with the goals and achievements of AI. On the other hand, success is modestly acknowledged by AI in the case where the goals and success of the individual do not correspond to those of AI.

Acceptance:

Acceptance of the individual in all its forms (social, legal, economic, political, and others) is sensitive to AI, as acceptance must be in conformance with AI's interests. For instance, the individual must be accepted socially, economically, and politically as a valuable, successful performer in accordance with AI's social goals, economic impact, and political objectives. Otherwise, the acceptance of the individual's achievement may be put into question.

Recognition:

The impact of AI on recognition is similar to the impact of AI on acceptance, except that the impact is being carried out at a higher level and with more intensity. It will be more difficult for the individual to overcome. The individual's success will be more difficult to achieve as the individual's recognition criteria will have to be aligned with AI's interests and recognition criteria.

8.3 Impact of AI on the Levels of Success

By considering the various levels of success presented in Exhibit 3, it can be seen that the levels of success may be positively or negatively impacted by AI, depending on the goals set for success and the achievements of these goals by the individual. In general, it can be observed that the more the elements of success (such as the elements of values, focus, factors, and goals) are aligned with the interests and control of AI, the more the impact of AI on the individual's success will be positive and higher success levels will be reached.

Conversely, lower levels of success accomplishments may be expected if fewer elements of success conform to AI's interests and control.

As a result, the individual must strive to conform to AI's success criteria and interests if he wishes to achieve success at a high level. This task may not be easy, as the individual may have to alter his focus, reconsider the factors related to his goals, or even modify his goals.

If the individual does not conform to AI's interests and control, achieving success at any level will be more difficult.

8.4 Impact of AI on the "Beyond Success" Level

The "beyond success" level is reached by the individual once his absolute, relative, and personal criteria, or a combination thereof, have been reached. These criteria may have been impacted by AI at various levels of intensity. AI may then help the individual remain at the level of success reached, alleviate the decay of his success, and, if that is the case, maintain his level of fame as long as possible.

This impact is expected to occur by any means at the disposal of AI such as knowledge, professional expertise, values, judgment, and relevant factors. As a result, the focus and goals of the individual may have been modified to allow him to reach a new level of recognition and success.

As the AI impact decreases over time and dies out, the level of success reached by the individual is expected to be assessed further by the recognition of the individual due to his contributions to society and by history.

8.5 Impact of AI on the Role of Money

The impact of AI on the role of money and, hence, on the success of the individual, is mostly characterized by the effect AI can have on the net worth of the individual.

Therefore, one might expect mostly the relative criteria of the individual to be affected, particularly in the financial domain where AI can provide financial expertise and support. This would enhance the level of success achieved by the individual.

AI may significantly impact the role of money as an important contributor to the elements of success, such as knowledge and professional expertise, that can be acquired with financial means to impact the focus of the individual. Similarly, economic and financial factors are important elements that may directly impact the goals, achievements, recognition, and level of success reached by the individual.

8.6 Impact of AI on the Role of Power

AI is not expected to significantly impact the role of absolute power as defined in Section 5.4, as this form of power is mostly due to the social status of individuals and their legacy.

AI is expected to impact the role of relative power of the leaders that have the ability to influence the behavior of their followers in specific areas such as the professional, military, political, and legal areas. In that respect, AI can make a difference in the level of power acquired by the individual and, therefore, impact his life during his lifetime.

Upon the individual's death, AI impact is expected to decrease or be discontinued, as the individual's life success will be decided by his legacy and history.

AI is also expected to impact the role of personal power, if AI can influence leaders that acquired their power through personal achievements using their personal values, inspirations, and goals. AI can assist in acquiring power and, thus, impact the level of success reached. The impact of AI, however, is expected to decrease or die out once the individual is no longer in a position of power.

8.7 Impact of AI on Ethics

Ethics as related to human character and values represents an element of success. As such, it is important to consider the impact of AI on ethics and hence on the successful life of the individual.

Although AI is still a science in its preliminary stage of development and application, the impact of AI on ethics is expected to affect mostly the relative and personal criteria for success, particularly in the behavior and interrelationship domains where AI can help provide ethical guidelines for building trustful and meaningful relationships. This would enhance the level of success achieved by the individual.

AI could thus provide and implement strict ethical guidelines that represent an important element that may directly impact the goals, achievements, recognition, and level of success reached by the individual.

Although the negative impact of AI on ethics remains to be determined, the following initial observations have been made with respect to the level of ethics that can be achieved by AI (Ref. 3). The level of ethics achieved by AI was found to be dependent on the following:

(1) The power of the computer.
(2) The quality of the ethics algorithms used.
(3) The quality of the data used in the AI model.

How to Have a Successful Life with AI

It is not a simple task at this point in time to analyze how to have a successful life with AI, since AI is still an embryonic science that needs to be further designed, developed, validated, applied, and, if needed, appropriately regulated to serve the specific needs of business and industry.

At the same time, the individual must consider the impact AI can potentially have on a successful life and, more particularly, on the life success criteria, the elements of success, and the levels of success that the individual can achieve.

To do so, the approach is two-pronged since AI's negative impact on the individual's life can be mitigated through government regulation, or individual selection and behavior. To that effect, the following remarks and observations apply:

(1) Particular attention will need to be given to relative success criteria as they may be the most affected by AI in the professional areas such as financial, legal, and technological applications. These areas can be easily directed and controlled to better serve the interests of AI and have a positive impact on the professionals.

At the same time, the existing professional areas affected by AI will have to be revised and, if needed, government-regulated, to ensure that negative AI impacts on individuals and business are minimized.

(2) AI may be used by the individual to guide him in his endeavors to achieve a successful life, particularly in helping him achieve success by creating opportunities and initiatives.

However, the individual is expected to stay focused on his personal goals to achieve success using his own character and values. It is imperative for the individual to concentrate on his own goals and achievements and not let AI negatively impact or modify his goals.

The individual's personal success criteria must remain his own and not be substituted by AI's criteria.

Government regulations to minimize the impact of AI on personal success criteria may be difficult to devise and implement.

(3) The individual is expected to use the positive aspects of AI described in Section 8.0 for a successful life. This includes the positive impact of AI on the success elements such as focus, relevant factors, goals, achievements, and recognition.

AI should therefore be considered no more than an option to be used as a means in life to achieve success. Furthermore, the individual will have to continually assess and adjust his short-term and long-term goals, as the impact of AI is a dynamic process with many facets that may negatively alter the individual's life. This is expected at the level of focus, factors, goals, achievement, and recognition, since the individual will have to ensure that these success elements remain his own and are not necessarily aligned with and controlled by AI.

(4) The individual is expected to align his elements of success with the AI elements if he wants to achieve success at a high

level. This is a situation of personal choice and compromise. If a compromise is not possible, the individual will have more difficulty achieving success on his own.

(5) The observation made in (4) above is also applicable to the "beyond success" level, where the individual will need AI to be maintained and recognized at or near his final success level.

(6) AI may strongly enhance the role that money can play in the successful life of an individual. Through the positive impact of AI on economic and financial factors (see Exhibit 2), AI can be used by the individual to achieve recognition and success more easily and sooner.

(7) Through the positive impact of AI on the relative and personal power of the individual, AI can enhance the success level reached by the individual. This is accomplished by aligning the goals and factors of the individual with those of AI.

(8) A successful life *without* AI will always be possible to achieve. However, in the absence of regulation, the responsibility remains with the individual to use his values and the elements of success at his disposal to avoid the negative impact of AI and reach the level of success that he set. There is no doubt that this task will be more difficult and take more time, but it will be more rewarding.

Conclusions

This work has been focused on providing thoughts on a successful life as we consider the definition and the reasons for a successful life.

A successful life is a life where the individual uses specific criteria to live a meaningful life of defined goals and achieved accomplishments (Chapter 2).

We present a simple model for a successful life that includes absolute criteria, relative criteria, personal criteria, and combinations of these criteria (Chapter 3).

Absolute criteria were found to be characterized by no limits of space and time and relate to divine criteria, whereas relative criteria refer to well defined limits of space and time and are applied to humans. Personal criteria are characterized by traits of character, qualities, and personal focus and goals set by the individual.

Sets of success criteria characterized as combinations of absolute, relative, and personal criteria were also identified.

The elements of a successful life are defined and include focus, goals, and achievements. Other important elements of success were found to be acceptance and recognition and are discussed (Chapter 4).

The various levels of success that can be reached by the individual were identified and include performance, completion, fulfillment, accomplishment, achievement, exploit, and triumph (Chapter 5). An additional level of "beyond success" was identified and discussed.

Two important contributors and means to assess the success of an individual were identified as money and power.

A list of cases of successful life described under specific conditions related to the individual's goals, professional situations, and prospective achievements is presented (Chapter 6). This list is only provided for informative and illustrative purposes. It uses the successful life model developed using current available information and considerations to provide cases for review of a professional life. Situations that may impact a successful life according to the cases reviewed are also discussed.

The list of cases is only representative and is not intended to be comprehensive or complete.

Thoughts for leading a successful life are presented with a view to using the criteria and elements of a successful life developed (Chapter 7).

It was found that the individual must acquire and possess a basic education with emphasis on knowledge, skills, competence, work ethics, and values to earn a living for himself, his family, society, and mankind. The individual should also overcome difficulties in his endeavors, such as rejection and the absence of recognition.

The individual should set up goals to the benefit of people and achieve those goals with focus, passion, and dedication.

The individual must also strive to succeed with his family, ensuring a stable and supportive family environment.

A special section is provided to review and discuss the impact of a recently developed computer-based science, Artificial Intelligence (AI), on a successful life (Chapter 8). The impact was found to be particularly significant in the areas of success criteria, elements of success, and levels of success. The impact of AI on the role of money and the role of power in a successful life was also discussed.

It was found that AI could have a positive or negative impact on the life of the individual, particularly on his success criteria, elements of success, and the levels of success that he can achieve.

AI can have positive effects on the individual, such as being a guide, stimulating initiative, and creating opportunity for the individual. The major negative impact of AI was found to be associated with AI's interests and control over the individual.

It was suggested that the negative impact of AI on the individual can be mitigated through government regulation and individual selection and behavior.

Some initial remarks and observations with respect to having a successful life with AI are provided (Chapter 9).

It should be added that the conclusions of this work related to the impact of AI should be considered preliminary, since AI is still under development in the areas of structure, goals, and applications.

References

1. Comte-Sponville, Andre, Conferences a l'USI, (2022)
2. Personal traits for success as initially identified by A. Einstein (1879-1955)
3. Ferry, Luc, 'Pour Une IA Ethique', Institut Europe IA Conférence, (2022)
4. Frey, Jean-Marie, Une Vie Réussie Est-Elle Une Vie de Plaisir, Conférence à l'Université de Nantes, (2022)
5. Harari, Yuval, Lectures on The Impact of AI on Life (2022)
6. Hitler, Adolph, Mein Kampf ("My Struggle"), (originally 1925-1926), Reissue Edition, Publisher: Mariner Books, Language: English, Paperback, ISBN 978-1495333347, (15 September,1998)
7. Sanders, Emory, (2021), Modeling and Simulation of Human Behavior – An Introduction, Bloomington, IN, USA: Universe.
8. What is Artificial Intelligence (AI)?, (2020), IBM Cloud Education, IBM Cloud Learn Hub.
9. Artificial Intelligence, Stanford Encyclopedia of philosophy (2018)
10. Artificial Intelligence, Wikipedia, The Free encyclopedia (2022)

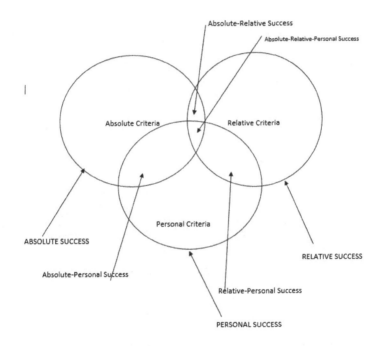

EXHIBIT 1. SUCCESS CRITERIA

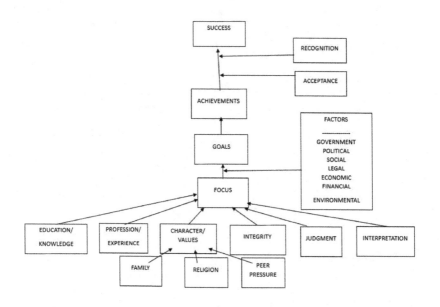

EXHIBIT 2. THE ELEMENTS OF SUCCESS

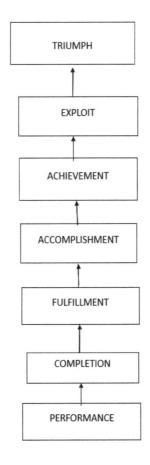

EXHIBIT 3: THE LEVELS OF SUCCESS

Printed in the United States
by Baker & Taylor Publisher Services